Naw Bì Ching

Modern Wisdom for Modern Problems

Jerry V. Behimino

Philipp Ines House

ISBN-13: 9798300215545

Cover design by: PI House Studio
Library of Congress Control Number: 2024924604
Printed in the United States of America

Contents

May timeless wisdom illuminate your journey,

Guiding you to embrace acceptance, release burdens,

And live authentically in harmony with yourself and the

universe.
~Naw Bì Ching

Preface

The great sages of old wrote in bamboo, silk, and silence.

Bolçi Tzu, however, wrote between email notifications, airport layovers, and the suspicious glare of public WiFi. He believed the Tao was timeless, but humans had grown glitchy.

Where ancient masters worried about ego and desire, modern seekers battle battery life, comparison culture, and the quiet dread of unread messages. Problems changed shape, but the human heart did not. It still longs for meaning, balance, and peace, even when it searches while scrolling.

In that spirit, *Naw Bì Ching: Modern Wisdom for Modern Problems* was born.

This book is not a parody of ancient wisdom. It is ancient wisdom translated through the lens of a digital-age wanderer, an observer of human contradictions, and the voice of Bolçi Tzu, a philosopher who never took himself too seriously, yet kept arriving at truth.

Across these pages are 81 reflections. They are not commandments and not doctrines. They are small openings.

Each chapter offers:
a simple parable
a quiet aphorism
a practical teaching rooted in acceptance, balance, and authenticity
Like the *Tao Te Ching*, these teachings are meant to be read slowly, returned to often, and understood differently each time your life changes.

You will find humor here, not to distract you, but to soften you.
You will find honesty, not to burden you, but to free you.
You will find simplicity, not because life is simple, but because clarity begins with one uncluttered step.

If this book helps you breathe deeper in a noisy world, choose gentleness where others choose force, or smile at the absurdity of being human in the twenty-first century, then Bolçi Tzu would say you have already begun to walk the Way.

May you read these teachings not as rules, but as reminders.
Peace is possible.
Wisdom is accessible.
Even in an age of algorithms and endless alerts, the ancient path is still beneath your feet.

Jerry V. Behimino
Humble student of life
Occasional translator of Bolçi Tzu

Exposition

Long before Bolçi Tzu wrote a single line of the *Naw Bì Ching*, he often remarked that the modern world had mastered the art of movement, but forgotten how to be still. People learned to connect across oceans, yet struggled to connect across a dinner table. They cultivated digital gardens of self-image while leaving their inner landscapes untended.

"Humans update their software," he said, "yet rarely update their souls."

With playful seriousness, Bolçi Tzu approached the wisdom of the Tao. He understood that ancient teachings are not fragile relics meant for museums. They are living philosophies meant to adapt, bend, and breathe with the times. In the age of scrolls, people read bamboo. In the age of screens, people scroll endlessly, searching for the same calm the ancients once sought beside rivers and mountains.

This reinterpretation is not a replacement of Lao Tzu and not a strict commentary. It is a companion for those navigating the chaos of modern life, a bridge between the serenity of timeless truths, the humor of human contradiction, and the realities of a world where the mind rarely unplugs.

Here you will find parables grounded in everyday life: signal bars on a phone, the illusion of perfection on social media, the tug-of-war between ambition and rest. Yet beneath their modern appearance, the pulse of the Tao remains. It is an invitation to live lightly, see clearly, act without force, and trust the rhythm of things.

Each chapter offers:

a story that is simple and disarming

an aphorism that distills its essence

a lesson that points gently toward balance

Some teachings will make you smile. Others may unsettle you. A few might reveal truths you already knew but forgot in the rush of staying busy.

Read as slowly as you wish, or as quickly as life demands. The wisdom is patient. It will meet you wherever you are.

May these reflections serve not as instructions, but as invitations. Pause. Breathe. Notice. Rethink.

Remember that the ancient path of harmony is still open, even in a world that hums with distraction.

The Way has never left us.
We simply learn to see it again.

On the Path of WiFi

The signal comes and goes. Your life does not need to chase it.

PARABLE:

In a small town, two friends set out in search of the legendary "perfect Wi-Fi signal."
Alice rushed from café to café, chasing full bars, refreshing apps that never stopped loading.
Bob wandered to the outskirts, where the connection was weak, but the silence was strong.
There, without notifications tapping at his mind, he found something surprising:
the world itself had more to say than any device he owned.
    Alice returned with screenshots.
Bob returned with clarity.

APHORISM:

"The stronger the signal, the weaker the stillness."

LESSON:

Connection isn't just about technology; it's about the relationships we cultivate. Prioritize real, meaningful interactions over constant connectivity.

The Art of Not Responding

Silence is a reply that protects your mind. Let urgency pass without you.

PARABLE:

A wise woman received a barrage of emails and notifications every day. Instead of replying hastily, she scheduled a "digital detox" week. When she returned, she found clarity. Most of the urgent messages had resolved themselves, and only the essential ones remained.

APHORISM:

"Silence speaks louder than screens."

LESSON:

Master the art of silence; not every notification demands your attention. Focus on what truly matters by filtering out the noise.

Embracing the Unfinished Project

8

Leave a corner unfinished so your soul can breathe. Completion is not the same as control.

PARABLE:

A woman began renovating her home but hesitated to finish, fearing it wouldn't be perfect. One day, a friend admired the "artistic chaos," and she realized her unfinished space was uniquely hers—a living canvas of creativity

APHORISM:

"Perfection is the enemy of completion"

LESSON:

Embrace imperfections; unfinished projects can lead to unexpected beauty and self-expression.

The Influence of FOMO

Miss more, find more. Presence beats curated highlights every time.

PARABLE:

A man lived in the grip of FOMO (Fear of Missing Out), endlessly scrolling through social media. One day, he turned off his phone and attended a local music festival. Immersed in live experiences, he found joy that no online feed could offer.

APHORISM:

"The more you miss, the more you find."

LESSON:

Authentic experiences outweigh the fear of missing out. Sometimes, the best moments happen when you're fully present.

Chapter Five

The Balance of Work and Play

14

Work is loud. Play is healing. Make room for laughter.

PARABLE:

A busy executive prioritized work over everything else, drowning in deadlines. One afternoon, the laughter of children playing outside his office window caught his attention. He joined them, rediscovering joy and returning to work rejuvenated.

APHORISM:

"Work hard but play harder."

LESSON:

Balance ambition with joy. Play isn't a luxury; it's essential for a healthy, productive life.

The Social Media Illusion

Unfiltered truth lands deeper than polished performance ever can.

PARABLE:

A young woman curated her life meticulously on social media, portraying an image of perfection. Feeling disconnected, she posted a candid photo of her messy living room. The genuine response from friends was overwhelming, sparking honest conversations and deeper connections.

APHORISM:

"Reality is better when unfiltered"

LESSON:

Authenticity resonates more than a polished image. Sharing your true self fosters genuine relationships.

Chapter Seven

Navigating Conflict with Calm

20

Offer tea before arguments. Let steam cool the ego.

PARABLE:

Two colleagues clashed over a project. Instead of escalating, one invited the other for coffee. Over warm mugs, they found common ground and turned conflict into collaboration.

APHORISM:

"Calm waters navigate troubled seas."

LESSON:

Approach conflict with patience and open communication. A calm demeanor can transform tension into understanding.

The Journey Inward

23

The map folds inward. Accept yourself and the search ends.

PARABLE:

An entrepreneur traveled the world seeking success yet felt unfulfilled. Reflecting one evening, she realized that no external achievement could fill her inner void. She began practicing mindfulness and discovered that self-acceptance was the real treasure.

APHORISM:

"The greatest journey is the one within."

LESSON:

Look inward for fulfillment; self-discovery is the path to true contentment.

Chapter Nine

Chronos vs. Kairos

Chronos ticks. Kairos opens. Time can be counted, meaning cannot.

PARABLE:

In a bustling city, a tech CEO was obsessed with time management, scheduling every minute. One day, he took a spontaneous walk and witnessed a street performer's act that moved him deeply. He realized that life's most meaningful moments aren't planned.

APHORISM:

"Time is a river; moments are the pearls."

LESSON:

Value quality over quantity. Embrace moments that bring joy rather than just filling your schedule.

Mastering the Mundane

29

The ordinary becomes sacred when you stop rushing through it. Let dust teach patience. Let mind settle.

PARABLE:

A barista found joy in crafting each cup of coffee, treating every order as an opportunity for artistry. Customers noticed his passion, and his café became a community hub.

APHORISM:

"Mundane tasks can harbor magic."

LESSON:

Find joy in everyday activities. Even simple tasks can be extraordinary when approached with love.

Chapter Eleven

The Garbage Collector's Wisdom

32

Clear the outside mess; the inside quiet follows.

PARABLE:

A young executive shadowed a sanitation worker to understand waste management. The worker shared, "Cleaning up the city's mess taught me to tidy up my own life."

APHORISM:

"*To tidy others is to tidy oneself.*"

LESSON:

By addressing external chaos, we often find clarity within ourselves.

The Nature of Change

35

Change is wind. Bend, release, and grow new leaves.

PARABLE:

A tech company resisted adopting new software, fearing disruption. Competitors embraced innovation and surged ahead. Realizing adaptability was key, the company updated its systems and regained its edge.

APHORISM:

"Adapt or be left behind."

LESSON:

Embrace change as an opportunity for growth. Resistance leads to stagnation.

Chapter Thirteen

The Joy of Letting Go

Let the balloon go. Sky keeps it better than fear.

PARABLE:

A woman held tightly to a vintage dress she never wore, cluttering her closet. One day, she donated it. Seeing someone else cherish the dress brought her unexpected happiness.

APHORISM:

"Holding on often weighs down the spirit."

LESSON:

Letting go creates space for new possibilities. Freedom from excess brings joy.

The Dangers of Overthinking

41

The sunset does not wait for your theories. Look up before the light fades.

PARABLE:

A man spent hours planning the perfect vacation but missed out on spontaneous adventures. His friend suggested they just go, leading to unexpected and memorable experiences.

APHORISM:

"Overthinking obscures clarity."

LESSON:

Embrace simplicity. Sometimes, the best experiences come without a plan.

The Beauty of Impermanence

Nothing lasts, so love it while it is here. Peace grows in acceptance of passing things.

PARABLE:

An artist created sand sculptures on the beach, knowing the tide would wash them away. Passersby asked why he bothered. He replied, "Their temporary nature makes them precious."

APHORISM:

"Impermanence gives beauty its value."

LESSON:

Cherish transient moments; their fleeting nature enhances their worth.

The Power of Non-Attachment

The splash fades, the lake remains. Be the still water.

PARABLE:

A tech enthusiast always had to have the latest gadgets. Realizing this constant chase left him unfulfilled, he decided to make the most of what he had. Free from the cycle of upgrades, he found contentment.

APHORISM:

"Attachments weigh the soul down like stones in water."

LESSON:

Letting go of constant desires frees us. Embrace the present without clinging to material possessions.

Chapter Seventeen

The Simplicity of Success

Success is quiet and close. It tastes like enough.

PARABLE:

An entrepreneur believed success meant luxury cars and high-end offices. After a health scare, he moved to a small town and started a modest business. He found joy in simplicity and community, redefining his idea of success.

APHORISM:

"Success is not measured by wealth, but by how deeply we enjoy life's simple gifts."

LESSON:

True success is found in embracing life's simple pleasures with gratitude.

Chapter Eighteen

Embracing Adaptability

53

The fist closes, the sand escapes. Open hand, keep peace.

PARABLE:

A software developer clung to outdated coding practices. Her projects lagged behind until she embraced new methodologies. By adapting, she stayed relevant and inspired.

APHORISM:

"Adaptability is the key to thriving in a world of constant change."

LESSON:

Be flexible in your approach. Adapting opens doors to growth and innovation.

Chapter Nineteen

The Wisdom of Waiting

Seeds grow on schedule, not demand. Trust the season.

PARABLE:

A startup founder rushed to launch his product, ignoring testing phases. The app failed due to glitches. His mentor advised patience. Taking the time to refine, his re-launched app succeeded.

APHORISM:

"Growth requires patience; you cannot rush the seasons."

LESSON:

Waiting teaches patience. Trust the process for lasting success

Chapter Twenty

The Mirror of Others

59

Clean the lens, not the landscape. Change the sky inside first.

PARABLE:

A social media influencer felt empty despite her followers. Volunteering at a community center, she saw genuine smiles reflected back at her. She realized fulfillment came from authentic connections, not online validation.

APHORISM:

"Your reflection in the world is a mirror of your heart."

LESSON:

How we perceive the world mirrors our inner state. Cultivate inner positivity to see it reflected externally.

Chapter Twenty-One

The Power of Small Acts

Drop one good pebble daily. Let the river carry it.

PARABLE:

A teenager started a neighborhood recycling program. Though small, it inspired others to join, leading to significant environmental impact.

APHORISM:

"Small acts of kindness create ripples that reach the farthest shores."

LESSON:

Never underestimate the impact of small actions. Collective small efforts lead to big change.

Chapter Twenty-Two

The Illusion of Security

65

Walls do not calm the mind. Build on practicing peace within, not a fortress.

PARABLE:

A man invested in high-tech home security, yet lived in fear. His neighbor, with no security system, felt safe and happy. Puzzled, the man asked why. The neighbor replied, "My security comes from trusting and knowing my community."

APHORISM:

"External security is a fleeting illusion; inner peace is the only true shield."

LESSON:

True security comes from within and our relationships, not just from external measures.

The Freedom of Non-Attachment

The cage may remain, but the struggle can end. Freedom begins in how you relate.

PARABLE:

A writer obsessed over reviews, letting criticism paralyze her. Deciding to write for herself, she released expectations. Her joy returned, and ironically, so did positive reviews.

APHORISM:

"True freedom comes not from escaping limitations, but from accepting them."

LESSON:

Release attachment to outcomes. Freedom lies in embracing the process, not fixating on results.

The Journey, Not the Destination

The journey teaches. Destinations are brief, lessons remain.

PARABLE:

A family road-tripped across the country, initially fixated on reaching their destination. Along the way, unplanned stops led to unforgettable experiences. They realized the trip itself was the real adventure.

APHORISM:

"The destination is but a stop; the journey is where wisdom resides."

LESSON:

Life isn't just about goals; it's about the experiences along the way. Embrace each moment.

The Power of the Pause

Stir less. Taste more. The soup will teach you.

PARABLE:

An overworked CEO scheduled back-to-back meetings. Burned out, she instituted "No Meeting Fridays." The pause boosted her team's creativity and productivity.

APHORISM:

"Pausing in life is not laziness; it's where wisdom is seasoned."

LESSON:

Taking breaks fosters creativity and clarity. Don't undervalue rest.

Chapter Twenty-Six

The Illusion of Control

The storm was never yours to command. Watch them, and soften inside.

PARABLE:

A project manager tried to micromanage every detail, leading to team frustration and project delays. Letting go, she trusted her team's expertise, resulting in a successful outcome.

APHORISM:

"The more you seek control, the more it slips away."

LESSON:

Control is often an illusion. Trust others and allow flexibility for better results.

Chapter Twenty-Seven

The Art of Listening

Hear the hush after speaking. Wisdom lives between words, not on them.

PARABLE:

During a brainstorming session, a team overlooked a quiet member. When they finally listened, her ideas revolutionized their project.

APHORISM:

"Wisdom is born in the quiet spaces where words cease to exist."

LESSON:

True wisdom comes from listening deeply. Make space for all voices.

The Foolish Pursuit of Perfection

Perfection polishes away the life. Let the rough edge be real.

PARABLE:

A photographer spent hours editing each image, missing deadlines. Challenged to post unedited photos for a week, he found that authenticity resonated more with his audience.

APHORISM:

"Perfection is a cage, not a crown."

LESSON:

Chasing perfection can hinder progress. Embrace authenticity over flawlessness.

Chapter Twenty-Nine

The Beauty of Solitude

Close the door gently. Meet the person inside it.

PARABLE:

Constant social engagements left Jenna exhausted. She planned a solo camping trip and rediscovered peace in solitude, returning rejuvenated.

APHORISM:

"Solitude is the canvas upon which we paint our true selves."

LESSON:

Time alone is essential for self-discovery. Embrace solitude as a means to reconnect with yourself.

The Strength of Flexibility

Bamboo bows and stays. Oak insists and falls. Bend and you endure.

PARABLE:

Constant social engagements left Jenna exhausted. She planned a solo camping trip and rediscovered peace in solitude, returning rejuvenated.

APHORISM:

"True strength lies in the ability to bend, not break."

LESSON:

Flexibility is a strength. Adaptability leads to resilience and success.

The Burden of Comparison

Stop measuring your sprouts. Tend your plot. Grow in your own soil, gently.

PARABLE:

Scrolling through social media, Liam felt inadequate compared to others' highlight reels. He decided to focus on his own journey, finding contentment in personal growth.

APHORISM:

"Comparison is a thief of joy."

LESSON:

Your path is unique. Focus on your own progress rather than comparing yourself to others.

Chapter Thirty-Two

The Power of Saying No

95

No is a boundary that protects your yes. Use it kindly.

PARABLE:

Overcommitted and stressed, Dina started declining additional responsibilities. Saying no allowed her to excel in her priorities and regain balance.

APHORISM:

"Freedom begins when you learn to say no."

LESSON:

Freedom begins when you learn to say no.

Chapter Thirty-Three

The Art of Doing Nothing

Doing nothing restores alignment. Stillness is productive medicine.

PARABLE:

Constantly busy, Alex felt unfulfilled. He scheduled an afternoon with no plans, allowing himself to relax. This unstructured time led to newfound creativity and happiness.

APHORISM:

"Sometimes, doing nothing is the most productive thing you can do."

LESSON:

Rest is vital. Unplanned time can lead to inspiration and rejuvenation.

The Mystery of the Present Moment

The secret was never hidden. The secret is now.

PARABLE:

During a family dinner, everyone was on their devices. Noticing this, the grandmother initiated a "no phones" rule at meals. Conversations flourished, and they cherished their time together.

APHORISM:

"Life is not a destination but the moment you're living."

LESSON:

Be present. Life's richness is found in the here and now.

Chapter Thirty-Five

The Paradox of Giving

Open your bowl. Abundance grows when expectations loosen.

PARABLE:

An online community member regularly shared knowledge freely. Her generosity built a reputation that led to unexpected opportunities and friendships.

APHORISM:

"The more you give, the more you grow."

LESSON:

Giving enriches both others and yourself. Generosity fosters connection and personal growth.

The Freedom of Simplicity

Fewer things, fewer chains. Own less so you can carry more peace.

PARABLE:

Tired of the rat race, David downsized his possessions and moved into a tiny house. With fewer distractions, he found more time for passions and relationships.

APHORISM:

"True freedom comes from owning less and living more."

LESSON:

Simplicity brings clarity and freedom. Let go of excess to focus on what truly matters.

Chapter Thirty-Seven

The Paradox of Non-Action

Stop paddling upstream. Stand aside and let flow do its work.

PARABLE:

Overwhelmed by environmental issues, a group decided to meditate together instead of protesting. Their peaceful approach inspired others to join, leading to a widespread movement of mindful living.

APHORISM:

"Non-action is the art of letting life do the heavy lifting."

LESSON:

Sometimes, stillness and reflection can lead to profound change. Allow space for solutions to emerge naturally.

Chapter Thirty-Eight

The Balance of Force and Softness

Feather moves air. Sword only cuts. Gentleness can move what strength cannot.

PARABLE:

In negotiations, a hardline executive always pushed aggressively, often losing deals. A colleague succeeded by listening and finding mutual benefits. The executive learned that a softer approach could yield better results.

APHORISM:

"Strength is in softness; power lies in flexibility."

LESSON:

Adapt your approach. Gentleness and understanding can be more effective than force.

Chapter Thirty-Nine

The Elusive Pursuit of Happiness

Stop chasing happiness. Sit still and it finds you

PARABLE:

Chasing promotions and accolades, Sarah never felt satisfied. Volunteering at a local shelter, she found joy in helping others, realizing happiness wasn't something to chase but to experience.

APHORISM:

"Happiness is not pursued but embraced when it arrives."

LESSON:

Happiness comes from meaningful experiences and connections. Be open to it in everyday moments.

The Dance of Light and Shadow

Stop arguing with your shadow. Add light and the whole picture changes.

PARABLE:

A filmmaker focused solely on dramatic, dark themes. His mentor suggested incorporating lighter moments. The resulting balance created a more impactful and relatable story.

APHORISM:

"Without light, shadows cannot dance."

LESSON:

Life is a balance of joy and sorrow. Embrace both to create depth and meaning.

The Gift of Vulnerability

When you leave no room for flaws, you leave no room for life.

PARABLE:

Sophia always maintained a flawless social media persona. One day, she shared her struggles openly. The support she received strengthened her relationships and self-acceptance.

APHORISM:

"True strength lies in the courage to be vulnerable."

LESSON:

Embrace vulnerability. Authenticity fosters deeper connections and personal growth.

The Power of Presence

Your body is here; Invite your mind to join it.

PARABLE:

Constant social engagements left Jenna exhausted. She planned a solo camping trip and rediscovered peace in solitude, returning rejuvenated.

APHORISM:

"Solitude is the canvas upon which we paint our true selves."

LESSON:

Time alone is essential for self-discovery. Embrace solitude as a means to reconnect with yourself.

The Wisdom of Patience

Waiting is not wasted. It is the soil doing its quiet work.

PARABLE:

An impatient chef rushed his recipes, resulting in mediocre dishes. Taking time to let flavors develop, his meals transformed, earning acclaim.

APHORISM:

"Patience turns seeds into trees."

LESSON:

Good things take time. Patience leads to quality and fulfillment.

Chapter Forty-Four

The Value of Stillness

Stillness is where skill ripens. Rest is part of the craft.

PARABLE:

A writer struggled with creativity until she spent a weekend unplugged in nature. The stillness sparked inspiration, and she completed her best work yet.

APHORISM:

"Stillness nurtures creativity."

LESSON:

Quiet moments fuel creativity and insight. Make time for stillness.

The Art of Acceptance

The fish come when they come. Stop fighting the now.

PARABLE:

After losing his job, Mark fought against his circumstances. Accepting the situation, he pursued a passion for woodworking, leading to a fulfilling new career.

APHORISM:

"Acceptance transforms waiting into living."

LESSON:

Accepting reality allows you to move forward and find new opportunities.

Chapter Forty-Six

The Value of Collaboration

Guide like water, not like chains. Flex don't force.

PARABLE:

Competing startups realized they shared a common goal. By collaborating, they combined strengths and created a groundbreaking product.

APHORISM:

"Collaboration multiplies success where competition divides it."

LESSON:

Embrace collaboration. Working together often leads to greater achievements.

The Quiet Strength

Roars scare others. Quiet strength endures.

PARABLE:

A musician let his work speak for itself. His genuine talent attracted a dedicated following without the need for fanfare.

APHORISM:

"True strength is quiet, not loud."

LESSON:

Authenticity and confidence often require fewer words. Let actions speak.

The Path of Least Resistance

Boulder stays. River moves. Efficiency without ego.

PARABLE:

An engineer insisted on using a complex solution when a simpler one sufficed. His colleague suggested an easier approach, saving time and resources.

APHORISM:

"Flow around obstacles. Resistance wastes energy and peace."

LESSON:

Don't complicate things unnecessarily. Sometimes, the simplest path leads to the best outcome.

The Power of Being

You were already enough. Sit down. Notice it.

PARABLE:

A mindfulness coach taught that instead of constantly doing, we should practice just being. Her students found peace and clarity by simply existing in the moment.

APHORISM:

"Wisdom isn't acquired. It's recognized when striving stops."

LESSON:

You already possess inner wisdom. Pause and allow it to surface.

The Paradox of Life and Death

The end is part of the pattern. Live fully because the page turns.

PARABLE:

A doctor working in palliative care learned that patients who embraced their mortality found more peace and meaning in their remaining time.

APHORISM:

"Life is brief. Live fully by releasing fear of endings."

LESSON:

Accept life's impermanence. Embracing mortality can enhance how fully we live

Chapter Fifty-One

The Subtle Art of Not Caring

Let judgments pass like wind. Keep your center.

PARABLE:

Emma constantly worried about others' opinions. Tired of the stress, she decided to live by her own values. She found freedom and attracted genuine relationships.

APHORISM:

"Stop renting peace to opinions. Protect your inner quiet."

LESSON:

Let go of the need for external approval. Authenticity brings peace.

The Illusion of Success

The ladder ends. The heart remains. Climb inward.

PARABLE:

A corporate lawyer achieved every career milestone but felt empty. Switching to a nonprofit role, he found fulfillment in contributing to a greater cause.

APHORISM:

"Success without fulfillment is like a river without water."

LESSON:

Redefine success beyond external achievements. Seek fulfillment and purpose.

Chapter Fifty-Three

The Dance of Chaos and Order

Stop choreographing life. Learn the rhythm of surprise.

PARABLE:

A graphic designer realized that her most creative work emerged when she allowed for spontaneity rather than sticking rigidly to plans.

APHORISM:

"Life is not meant to be controlled; it is meant to be experienced."

LESSON:

Embrace the balance between structure and spontaneity. Allow room for the unexpected.

The Power of Surrender

Float for a while. The river knows valleys you don't.

PARABLE:

Facing burnout, a startup founder stepped back and entrusted his team. Letting go led to innovative ideas and revitalized the company.

APHORISM:

"Sometimes, the strongest move is to surrender."

LESSON:

Surrendering control can lead to empowerment and fresh perspectives.

The Power of Forgiveness

164

Accept cracks and flaws. Worry shrinks joy into dust.

PARABLE:

After a falling out, two friends avoided each other. One decided to extend an olive branch. Forgiving and reconciling brought relief and restored their friendship.

APHORISM:

"Forgiveness frees the heart."

LESSON:

Let go of grudges. Forgiveness heals and allows you to move forward.

Chapter Fifty-Six

The Joy of Imperfection

Butterfly finds the crack. Stop building thicker fear.

PARABLE:

JR, an artist, joined a daily sketch challenge, creating without overthinking. His spontaneous art resonated more than his meticulous pieces.

APHORISM:

"Perfection is found in embracing imperfections."

LESSON:

Accept imperfections to unleash creativity and authenticity.

The Wisdom of the Fool

The wise stay curious. Humility keeps you learning.

PARABLE:

A newcomer at a tech firm asked simple questions that others overlooked. His fresh perspective led to innovative solutions.

APHORISM:

"True wisdom is in the humility of not knowing."

LESSON:

Stay curious and open minded. Acknowledging what you don't know fosters growth.

Chapter Fifty-Eight

The Strength of Community

Too many treasures, too many chains. Carry less.

PARABLE:

After a natural disaster, neighbors organized relief efforts. Their collective action rebuilt the community faster than any individual could.

APHORISM:

"Community turns strangers into allies."

LESSON:

Foster community bonds. Together, we are stronger and can overcome great challenges.

The Freedom of Silence

Turn down the world. Hear your breath's advice.

PARABLE:

Attending a silent retreat, Maya found that without speaking, she became more attuned to her thoughts and emotions, gaining profound insights.

APHORISM:

"Silence is not the absence of noise; it is the presence of peace."

LESSON:

Embrace silence to connect with your inner self. It offers clarity and tranquility.

The Art of Living in the Moment

Stop polishing the door. Walk through it today.

PARABLE:

Photographing a concert, Jason realized he was experiencing life through a lens. Putting down the camera, he immersed himself in the music, creating a lasting memory.

APHORISM:

"Life is happening now, not in the future."

LESSON:

Be present. Fully engage with the moment rather than trying to capture or plan it.

The Power of Inner Calm

Don't stir the pond. Wait. The bottom becomes visible.

PARABLE:

During a city-wide blackout, while others panicked, Elora lit candles and enjoyed a quiet evening. Her calm demeanor inspired her neighbors to relax and make the best of the situation.

APHORISM:

"Calmness is the art of stilling the mind amidst the storm."

LESSON:

Cultivate inner peace. Your calm can positively influence those around you.

The Power of Gratitude

Drop one gentle act. Watch circles widen on water.

PARABLE:

Rasheed shifted from feeling inadequate to writing daily gratitude entries. This practice transformed his outlook, leading to increased happiness.

APHORISM:

"Gratitude turns what we have into enough."

LESSON:

Practice gratitude to find contentment and joy in the present.

The Impact of Mindfulness

Sit with one breath. Thoughts pass like e-bikes. Do not chase.

PARABLE:

Rachel incorporated mindfulness into her hectic routine. This small change reduced her stress and improved her relationships.

APHORISM:

"Mindfulness turns moments into meaningful experiences."

LESSON:

Be present in daily activities. Mindfulness enhances well-being.

Chapter Sixty-Four

The Benefits of Physical Activity

Move your body daily, the heart clears, the mind steadies.

PARABLE:

Sedentary and uninspired, Tom started daily walks. The physical activity boosted his mood and creativity.

APHORISM:

"A healthy body nurtures a healthy mind."

LESSON:

Engage in regular exercise to improve both physical and mental health.

Chapter Sixty-Five

The Freedom of Minimalism

194

Own less, need less; your days widen, your mind quiets.

PARABLE:

Anna decluttered her life, letting go of unnecessary possessions. The simplicity brought clarity and peace.

APHORISM:

"Less is more when it brings you peace."

LESSON:

Simplify to focus on what truly matters. Minimalism can lead to greater fulfillment.

The Art of Self-Care

Tend your body like a small garden. Water first, then speak.

PARABLE:

Princess prioritized self-care, setting boundaries and nurturing her well-being. This empowered her to be more present and effective.

APHORISM:

"Taking care of yourself is not selfish; it's essential."

LESSON:

Self-care is vital. Nurture yourself to better handle life's demands.

The Power of Now

Return from tomorrow. Sit in this breath. Let it be enough.

PARABLE:

Constantly planning for the future, Eugene missed out on present joys. He began practicing mindfulness, finding happiness in the current moment.

APHORISM:

"The present moment is the gateway to all wisdom."

LESSON:

Embrace the now. The present is where life truly happens.

The Wisdom of Silence

Choose silence sometimes; it protects truth from needless noise.

PARABLE:

In meetings, Sarah started listening more and speaking less. This shift led to deeper understanding and better solutions.

APHORISM:

"Silence speaks the truth that words cannot reach."

LESSON:

Value silence. It allows you to truly hear and understand others.

The Paradox of Strength and Weakness

Strength can yield; Yielding is not losing.

PARABLE:

In a debate, a leader admitted he didn't have all the answers. His vulnerability earned respect and opened collaborative dialogue.

APHORISM:

"True strength is found in yielding, not in force."

LESSON:

Embrace vulnerability. Strength often lies in acknowledging weaknesses.

Chapter Seventy

The Power of Empathy

Listen like you might be wrong; kindness changes everything.

PARABLE:

AJ improved his team's morale by practicing empathy, leading to better collaboration and success.

APHORISM:

"Empathy bridges understanding and builds unity."

LESSON:

Understand others' perspectives. Empathy strengthens relationships.

Chapter Seventy-One

Environmental Stewardship

212

Leave places better; what you protect also protects you.

PARABLE:

Communities initiated local environmental projects, collectively making a significant impact on combating climate change.

APHORISM:

"Protect the earth, and it will protect you."

LESSON:

Take responsibility for the environment. Individual actions matter.

Chapter Seventy-Two

The Joy of Lifelong Learning

215

Stay curious; learning keeps your spirit young and unafraid.

PARABLE:

Maria found renewed purpose by learning new skills, enriching her life post-retirement.

APHORISM:

"Learning keeps the spirit young."

LESSON:

Embrace continuous learning for a fulfilling life.

The Power of Resilience

Stay curious; learning keeps your spirit young and unafraid.

PARABLE:

Maria found renewed purpose by learning new skills, enriching her life post-retirement.

APHORISM:

"True strength lies not in avoiding hardship but in how we rise from it."

LESSON:

Embrace setbacks as opportunities to grow stronger.

Stay curious; learning keeps your spirit young and unafraid.

PARABLE:

Maria found renewed purpose by learning new skills, enriching her life post-retirement.

APHORISM:

"Learning keeps the spirit young."

LESSON:

Embrace continuous learning for a fulfilling life.

The Paradox of Effort

223

Stop muscling the door. Turn the knob gently.

PARABLE:

A salesperson relaxed his hard-sell tactics and focused on genuine conversations. His sales increased naturally.

APHORISM:

"Effortless effort leads to greater success."

LESSON:

Don't force outcomes. Authentic efforts often yield better result

The Trap of Wanting More

Wanting more keeps you empty; gratitude fills you right now.

PARABLE:

Despite wealth, Lisa felt empty. Volunteering abroad, she found fulfillment in simplicity and service.

APHORISM:

"Wanting more keeps us empty; contentment fills the soul."

LESSON:

Contentment comes from appreciating what you have, not accumulating more.

Embracing Uncertainty

Uncertainty is normal; relax your grip and adapt gracefully.

PARABLE:

Joey stepped out of his comfort zone by accepting a job abroad, leading to unexpected growth.

APHORISM:

"Life begins at the edge of your comfort zone."

LESSON:

Embrace the unknown. Growth often comes from new experiences.

Chapter Seventy-Seven

The Paradox of Change

232

Say yes to the present. The next step reveals itself.

PARABLE:

Accepting her company's restructuring, Nohemy found new opportunities within, rather than resisting the change.

APHORISM:

"Change begins with acceptance, not resistance."

LESSON:

Accept change to move forward. Resistance hinders growth.

The Value of Diversity

Different voices strengthen us; many colors make one cloth.

PARABLE:

Diverse teams at a tech company produced innovative solutions, highlighting the strength in varied perspectives.

APHORISM:

"Diversity is the catalyst for innovation."

LESSON:

Embrace diversity. It enriches understanding and creativity.

Chapter Seventy-Nine

The Art of Digital Detox

Dim the screen-glow. Let your eyes return to sky.

PARABLE:

Liam unplugged for a weekend, rediscovering connection with himself and others

APHORISM:

"Disconnect to reconnect."

LESSON:

Take breaks from technology to rejuvenate your mind and relationships.

The Beauty of Uncertainty

The unknown can open doors; step through before fear decides.

PARABLE:

When her company downsized, Kathleen saw it as an opportunity to start her own business, leading to greater fulfillment.

APHORISM:

"Embrace the unknown to find your true path."

LESSON:

Uncertainty can lead to new beginnings. Welcome it as a catalyst for growth.

Chapter Eighty-One

The End of the Beginning

244

Every ending opens a door; step forward without clinging.

PARABLE:

At his graduation, a student realized that learning was a lifelong journey, not confined to classrooms.

APHORISM:

"There is no end, only new beginnings."

LESSON:

Every ending is a new start. Embrace life's continuous cycle of growth

Afterword

In Naw Bì Ching: Modern Wisdom for Modern Problems, we have delved into contemporary challenges through the lens of timeless truths. Each chapter has underlined the importance of inner peace and success through acceptance, letting go, and authenticity rather than through constant striving, controlling, or accumulating.

Empowering Lessons for a Modern Life.

Prioritize Connection: Foster real relationships that provide depth and meaning well beyond the digital connections that dominate today's landscape.

Value Authenticity: Embrace your true self for a deeper, more fulfilling journey through life.

Seek Balance: Find harmony between work and leisure, effort and relaxation, enriching your days with a well-rounded existence.

Adapt and Evolve: Embrace change as not just inevitable but as a positive force that propels you forward.

Cherish Moments: Discover the true richness of life in experiences and interactions rather than material possessions.

Armed with these insights, you are now better equipped to navigate the complexities of modern life. May this book serve as your compass, guiding you toward a life filled with joy, balance, and authenticity in an ever-changing world.

About the author

Jerry V. Behimino writes modern parables that blend philosophical insight with practical, usable guidance. In *Naw Bì Ching*, he explores how to keep balance and inner calm in a world shaped by digital noise, social pressure, and constant urgency. Across 81 short chapters, he returns to a simple thesis: peace and success come less from striving and more from acceptance, restraint, and authentic living.

Drawing on a multicultural, adaptable perspective and a deep interest in global human stories, Jerry's work carries a quiet attentiveness to place and atmosphere. Japan's history and everyday stillness continue to influence his approach, shaping a voice that is reflective, direct, and occasionally wry.

Naw Bì Ching invites readers to navigate modern complexity with ancient wisdom, contemporary clarity, and a gentle sense of humor.

www.ingramcontent.com/pod-product-compliance
Lightning Source LLC
Chambersburg PA
CBHW051552250726
48653CB00004BA/1111